ALISON WEM

# Never Feel Alone

*Step-by-step guide to connect with your passed loved ones, soul and spirit guides for healing and support, clarity and personal growth*

*First edition*

*ISBN: 978-1-9997014-7-5*

*This book was professionally typeset on Reedsy.*
*Find out more at reedsy.com*

*In Loving Memory*

*Of*

*Paula Barder, a dear friend and mentor.*

Solitude is my home.

Loneliness was my cage.

Renuka Gavrani

# Contents

# Foreword

Paula Barder, friend and mentor, inspired the writing of this book, Never Feel Alone. It was something she said to me many times. Outwardly bright and gentle, she held within a soul of great strength and compassion albeit sometimes fierce if crossed. This soul carried Paula through her childhood illnesses and would not accept a life living with disability in a wheelchair. At our last meeting, when she was in her 90s, Paula was proud that she could still stand on her own two feet in every sense.

Spirit put us together when I needed to talk about my experiences in my inner landscape. Paula said I was like a hot kettle on the hob about to explode! For many years I had explored my inner landscape by just following my intuition. I never spoke to anyone of my adventures for fear of being considered weird. Sharing my inner adventures with Paula, together we gained a better understanding of what was happening and I gained greater perspective on my life's purpose. Paula was and is a professional listener par excellence.

I always knew Paula was busy helping 'her people' but it was not until her passing, did I realise, just how many people's lives she had touched. She has been of great service to so many, strengthening and healing their relationship with their inner self, their soul and bringing peace where anguish had once dwelt.

I believe Paula continues to guide people in need of support. I received a message only today via a friend encouraging me to call myself a 'Spiritual Teacher.' She sent the message indirectly as she knew I would question it if she spoke to me directly. Her last words to me in this lifetime were "Get yourself out there and share your wisdom and messages." I am listening Paula.

Paula gave her all to her Earthly life and continues to do so.

Well done, Paula. A life well lived.

Love,

Alison Wem

Spiritual Teacher

# Introduction

Loneliness arrived at my door swiftly and unexpected one winter's evening. My husband and I had planned to go away for the weekend to celebrate our 25th wedding anniversary. The children were already at my mum's house so we could go to a wonderful hotel with just the two of us. On Friday in the late afternoon, I received a call at work that my husband had been taken ill and I should come home quickly. I arrived to the ambulance in our drive way with the blue light flashing. My husband was being taken to hospital and I should follow in my car. I went into hospital with a husband and came out in the early hours of the morning with just his wedding ring. I stood in the car park feeling overwhelmed. I remember the coldness of the night and the stars twinkling above my head and looking at the ring in the palm of my hand. I had thought we would grow old together but now I had to go and tell our children we no longer had their dad with us. How was I going to do that? It was the first step in a long hard road of rebuilding my life with loneliness as my main companion.

Some would say I was lucky to have my children, which of course I was. But I came to crave adult company. I had a great desire to be hugged by someone my own size who loved me for who I was.

I came to realise that loneliness comes from that uncomfortable feeling when there is a gap between your desire for social connection and your actual experience of it. I had a busy life and was surrounded by people all day; getting children to school, doing my job, being with the children in the evenings and weekends. Yet I still felt a deep and pervasive loneliness. I had lost my companion in life who I had known since I was seventeen. I thought I was a confident, outward going person but alone I felt weak, shy and uninteresting. I no longer knew who I was.

Loneliness should not be confused with self-imposed solitude. Some people enjoy being on their own. With it can come a sense of freedom to do exactly as they wish. For those who value this over everything else, being on their own is a gift and they don't feel lonely.

For me now in my rebuilt life, periods of solitude are a gift. I use them when I want to write a book or to just be with me and my soul. I feel both energised and calmed by it and can return to the world and enjoy the full rigours of life.

However, it wasn't always like this. I did a lot of reflection on myself and who I really am to get to the point of enjoying isolation. It should be recognised that loneliness is one of the worst human conditions. We are tribal by nature. So, if you feel lonely, don't be cross with yourself, be kind. Treat yourself as a loving friend would.

Besides widowhood, there are many other triggers for loneliness, some of which go unseen. Divorce is a common trigger for loneliness. It can be made harder if it comes with a sense of failure to make the relationship work or humiliation in what happened in the relationship. These emotions can increase loneliness as it is harder to take action to get back into the world.

Even within a long-term partnership there can be a sense of loneliness. The person you fell in love with twenty years ago may not be the person you live with now. Sadly, nothing stands still.

Even people who look highly successful may be experiencing loneliness. They may have put so much energy into their careers that their home life is barren. They missed the opportunity to participate in their children growing up. Their marriage may be carried out without real interest, feeling, or effort.

Loss of easy contact with family and friends perhaps through a geographical relocation can bring about loneliness. Children going to university for the first time often experience their first feelings of loneliness.

Loneliness is not restricted to the old. It can happen at any time in your life. For some it creeps up on them over time. You can fall into loneliness without intending to.

The big question is – *What should you do about your loneliness?*

If you Google, what should I do about my loneliness, many suggestions will come back on how to increase your opportunities for social interaction. This book aims to give you another perspective on how to tackle your loneliness. You are lonely for a reason but quite possibly it is not the trigger causing it. For me, my trigger was being widowed. But the real reason was that I did not have sufficient internal resources to weather that situation without a protracted period of loneliness. It was that feeling of loneliness that drove me to look at myself in the face and decide who I was.

*Did I want to be a grieving widow for the rest of my life?*

No! I wanted to have fun, laugh and enjoy my life.

*What did I want to change so I could enjoy my life again?*

I wanted my husband and old life back but that wasn't possible. My dilemma was I didn't know myself sufficiently to know what would feel like fun and make me laugh when it was just me doing it. I really didn't know myself that well even though I was in my mid-40s.

This thought set me on a voyage of discovery. It wasn't a direct journey from A to B. I wondered around trying things out. I allowed myself to be led by my own feeling of what was right for me. Some people call that your 'gut feeling'. Now I realise it was my intuition gently guiding me. I didn't know anything about intuition then, but I did know what felt good to me. I followed that feeling resolutely.

Before you follow Google's advice on tackling loneliness, I would encourage you to get to know yourself better. Without this wisdom, you may have many wasted efforts to resolve your loneliness.

This book aims to give you another perspective on loneliness and how you might get to know the real you.

# 1

# The Gift of Loneliness

I asked my friend and mentor who was a single lady in her 90s living alone, if she ever felt lonely. Her immediate reply was – Never. I came to realise she knew exactly what she wanted to do with her life and was boldly getting on with it. Loneliness was not part of it. A love of music, care for others and helping others to get the most out of their lives were her main drivers for living. Since her passing, I have found out how many peoples' lives she has touched and how much she was loved. She lived a good life with purpose. There was no space for loneliness to creep in.

*What would a good life look like to you and what would be your purpose?*

The answer to that question can come in many ways. Some will be framed by your trigger, such as a sense of freedom after a controlling relationship. However, to answer truthfully you need to know yourself well. It needs to be from the core or you and not just a reaction to your trigger.

So rather that hating what has happened to you, come to accept it is an opportunity for you to change your life to be what makes you feel good. Not what anyone else desires for you. But what you want.

My good friend Dee was diagnosed in her early 30s with breast cancer. Her life changed dramatically. Pre-diagnosis, she had a full life with a blossoming career, outings with lots of friends, holidays in the sunshine. Post diagnosis, her life was constrained to undergoing cancer treatment with limited contact with people to protect her from germs due to a compromised immune system. Dee felt lonely and not at all happy.

Dee decided not to allow her illness to define who she was. Her career was in the medical arena so she decided to take control of her treatment. She researched the proposed treatment especially the side effects. Dee was keen to retain her fertility as she was wanting to have a family post treatment. The hospital soon learnt not to give Dee a treatment unless she had fully understood it and agreed to it.

In her personal life, Dee decided to make her research known to other women who might not have a medical background. From this she was invited by a charity to represent Berkshire in a fashion show with cancer patients as the models. Dee was invited to give a speech to represent her follow patients' views on life. This was such an inspirational speech Dee has been invited on talk shows, initially at county level but now at national level.

Far from feeling isolated and lonely, Dee's life is full of purpose and service to other women experiencing life threatening cancer. She has re-defined who she is and from that found a new path through her life. She is positively blooming when she could have been wilting.

My experience is that it takes personal isolation to explore your inner landscape. It doesn't mean you need to stay for a week in a cabin in the forest on your own. But you do need time and space to consider your answer on what feels 'good' for you. A quiet corner of your home where you will not be interrupted is a good place to choose.

Maddy, who is one of my clients, chose her bathroom. She said it was the only room in a busy household which only she went in. It has become her reflection room and only contains her desires and energy.

Through reflecting on this question of what feels good for you, you will start to enter your inner landscape. It sometimes helps to close your eyes and to take some deep breaths. Your inner landscape is the place inside you where you find not chaos and more pain but a space of calmness and a route to strength, love and guidance.

Just taking the action to do this reflection a number of times can help you to focus on something other than your loneliness. This in itself is beneficial. However, most people find it opens a whole new vista on themselves.

For me as a widow it happened intuitively in the early morning twilight hours when unable to sleep, I was driven inside asking the question – there has to be more to life than this unending sadness and loneliness? To my surprise and delight, I felt a sense of being loved.

Of course, this was only the very early start of a much longer journey. A journey which has made me who I am today. I count my blessings that I fell in love again and my husband came with a large, boisterous and loving family. We celebrate our 20th wedding anniversary this year. I successfully raised my children to become happy, caring and successful adults and was given the opportunity to assist in the growing of my step-children. I gave up corporate life and its income as I valued the time and energy to progress what was important to me. Today I am a spiritual teacher of dreams, healing and psychic mediumship. My life today couldn't be more different from my life when I was widowed.

I am an ordinary person. I am not more special than anyone else. I am only telling you about my transformation because if I can do it, so can you. It was from exploring my inner landscape that I met my soul and my guides who helped to nurture me back to life. Spirit guides are spiritual entities that offer guidance, support and wisdom. Many people report their guides are serious and authoritative. This was not my experience. They became my friends and they have a sense of humour. When I was down, they helped to lift me up. When I presented them with my best efforts, they were never critical but were very pleased I had tried. They then went on to suggest what else I could do. But in so doing I felt listened to, loved and nurtured.

I would encourage you to see the mishap of your loneliness as a wake-up call to find your real self and to go on to live a happy life with who you really are.

*The journey through your inner landscape goes on to the day you die. It can be fun, exciting, insightful, ease pains you did not know you were carrying and also healing emotionally and physically.*

Besides getting to know your own soul and spirit guides, you get the opportunity to meet with passed loved ones. There are many reasons for meeting with a loved one. Often it is just to feel their love or they may want an update on the family. It can also be for a particular reason such as to give advice on something in your life or to resolve some unfinished business.

Amy, a colleague, told me about meeting with her father-in-law in a dream, after he had passed, to resolve some unfinished business. She spoke to me about it to ask if I thought it was a real encounter or wishful thinking on her behalf. Having listened to her story, I felt it was very much real. I am a believer that life goes on after we pass. We are just in a different physical state. We take our loves and cares into the Afterlife with us to help us to learn.

Amy's father-in-law, William, passed at the grand age of 98. He was much loved by his family but had only enjoyed limited contact in his later years due to the pandemic of 2020. During the pandemic his daughter and son-in-law were part of his family bubble. They lived some way away so could not visit him every day. His daughter organised his food to be delivered and with some help from neighbours checked he was physically alright each day. Pre-pandemic Amy was a regular visitor of her father-in-law and loved him deeply. However, she and his son lived in a city and were afraid to visit during the pandemic for fear of bringing germs to his door. After the pandemic, Amy planned to have a conversation with her William about the absence of recent visits from his son and herself. However, he passed before she was able to have this conversation with him. She was left with a feeling of sadness that he may have felt we did not love him.

In the dream Amy met with William, he took her to the top of a hill on a beautiful Mediterranean island. The sun was shining and the sea was a rich sparkly blue. Amy felt the setting was a reminder of the great holidays she and her husband had taken William on since he was widowed. On the top of the hill there was a single tree. In the shade of the tree was a table and two chairs. On the table was an open bottle of red wine and two glasses waiting for them. It was just what they used to do of an evening on their happy family holidays. William and Amy sat down together, drank a glass of wine and had a good chat. They sorted out any misunderstanding. Amy left the dream feeling much happier knowing William understood they loved him.

*Are you ready to take the first step to connect with your spirit messengers?*

All you need to know now are the actions to open the door to your inner landscape. Accepting the opportunity you are being offered, will help you to discover strength, hope and confidence to relaunch your life to a happier place.

# 2

# Simple Signals of Communication From Your Guides

Your soul and guides are continually trying to get in touch with you. These simple signals are the most common way in which people receive messages. They offer you guidance, support and wisdom. Your soul holds all of the wisdom you have ever earned through living. However, the communication can be very subtle and you need to be looking out for it not to miss the messages. Some of the ways they will use to connect with you are;

- **Intuitive insights**
- **Synchronicity**
- **Physical sensations**
- **Signs in nature**

- **Auditory signals**
- **Visual signs**
- **Messages through others**
- **Finding and moving objects**
- **Feeling a presence**
- Dreams and visions.

Let's expand on each of these to give a better understanding.

## Intuitive Insights

These come in the form of 'Gut Feelings' sudden strong feelings or gut instincts about a situation, person or decision. Or 'Inner Knowing', a deep sense of certainty about something without logical reasoning.

## Synchronicity

Meaningful coincidences such as repeatedly encountering specific numbers, symbols, or events that seem too coincidental to be random. A series of synchronicity events are often a nudge to take your life in a certain direction. I believe my friend Dee, we spoke of earlier, had received such a phenomenon which changed the course of her life.

Other synchronicity include patterns and repetition such as seeing the same numbers (like 11:11), hearing the same song, or encountering the same phrase repeatedly.

## Physical Sensations

Feeling chills or goosebumps often in response to a particular thought or situation. This particularly happens to me when I am working with a client and something I have relayed from their guide really hits the mark. My client will often experience it too.

Other people may tend to feel tingling or warmth, especially in the hands, feet, or top of the head. I have found that the area of the third eye chakra between your brows and the crown chakra at the top of your head can become warm when you are strongly connecting with spirit messengers.

We are all different as are our guides. So be alert to how your guide consistently chooses to emphasis messages with you.

## Signs in nature

This can be through animals and weather patterns. Encountering specific animals, especially ones that appear repeatedly or in unusual circumstances. Or experiencing changes in weather (like sudden breezes or rainbows) at significant moments.

## Auditory signals

Typically these include hearing a voice or sound in your mind that provides guidance or reassurance. Although voice is often expected, in my experience hearing a voice is quite unusually. Other signs tend to be more common. A common auditory sign is hearing specific songs or lyrics that resonate deeply or provide answers to your questions.

For me, the most notable example I can remember of a word communication was when our beloved cat was taken ill. My daughter and I stayed up with him all night. In the morning when I picked him up, my guide distinctly said in my head "Your cat has had his last night on Earth," The use of words surprised me a great deal as we usually communicated telepathically. I can only suggest he wanted me to be absolutely clear on the message so he used words. The clarity of the message helped me to know how to handle my little girl and her emotions. She loved her cat so much, especially since she had lost her dad.

## Visual signs

Such as seeing flashes or orbs of light often in your peripheral vision. This is less common than some signs but significant when it happens. Some of my clients can be initially a little wary of what they are seeing. However, when they relax the orbs can come with important wisdom

Another and perhaps more common visual sign is seeing specific symbols, numbers, or images that have personal significance.

## Messages through others

Such as unexpected advice or guidance from strangers or acquaintances that seems particularly relevant. A common approach seems to be to receive guidance through books whose content provides answers or insights into your challenge or situation. Personally, I read all of the books my guide sends across my path. When I'm browsing in a book shop, either a physical or online one, it might simple be a book that jumps out at me and says - Read Me!

## Finding objects and moving objects

This includes discovering objects (like feathers, coins, or crystals) in unusual places or at significant times. Plus noticing objects being moved or placed in a way that seems intentional.

## Feeling a Presence

Sensing a comforting or supportive presence around you, especially during times of need.

## Dreams and visions

As a dream teacher this is a particular passion of mine. There does seem to be an increasing interest in dreaming along with the interpretation of the dreams. Perhaps it's because everyone dreams even though you may or may not remember them. Or perhaps you remember a fragment of a dream. They create a bridge between your inner and outer worlds. Many believe that dreams are not just random images but meaningful messages of love and guidance from your soul.

Understanding your dreams can offer profound insights from your inner world, guiding you on your life journey.

Dreams can be vivid or vague, joyful or terrifying, linear or chaotic, fantastic or ordinary. Despite their varied nature, dreams often carry symbols to guide you in your life or to give you an alert to a possible danger ahead.

How are your soul and guides trying to speak to you in your dreams?

Here are some of the things you should be alert to in your dreams to aid understanding them.

**How do you feel when you wake up?**

Emotions you experience in dreams are significant. Waking feeling curious may mean there is something from your dream you need to research and explore further. If you frequently feel anxious in dreams, it could be a sign that your soul is urging you to address anxiety-inducing aspects of your life. Dreams can bring you happiness in meeting a loved one who has passed. Every human emotion can be experienced in dreams.

**Symbolic Dreams**

Dreams are rarely communicated in a straightforward way. Instead, they use symbols that require interpretation. Examples can include; water symbolising emotions, a house could represent yourself, and a journey might reflect personal growth. Paying attention to recurring symbols can help you decode the messages your soul is sending. A repeated dream can often mean there is a message your soul is trying to give you, but you have not understood it yet.

**What guidance and clarity are your dreams bringing you?**

Dreams can provide guidance and clarity on issues that perplex you. They might offer solutions to problems, reveal new perspectives, or confirm gut feelings. When you have a problem, many people like to sleep on it before they take any actions.

A dream about a crossroads, for example, could symbolize a critical decision you need to make. Dreams can sometimes predict potential futures and alert you to avoiding accidents or harm.

**Healing Dreams**

Your soul uses dreams to facilitate healing. Traumatic experiences or unresolved conflicts often resurface in dreams, giving you a chance to process and heal. The healing dream can be symbolic with you as a wounded animal walking to a blue lake for healing and diving in. Confronting these issues in the dream world can lead to emotional release and closure.

**Dream visits from loved ones and spirit guides**

These are perhaps my favourite dreams. I always feel very loved in these dreams and a wonderful feeling of being connected to the people most important to me.

These dream visits are a great opportunity to complete unfinished business or sort out misunderstandings with a passed loved one.

Meaningful discussions can be held with spirit guides to help you with an aspect of your life or spiritual development.

**How do you improve your dream communications?**

- **Keep a Dream Journal,** in my experience the more you write of your dreams in a journal in the morning, the more dreams you receive. It's like you are saying you are open to dream communication.
- **Practice Mindfulness and meditation,** it seems to improve dream recall, perhaps because you have greater inner calmness.
- **Set Intentions,** before you go to sleep write an intention or question in your journal for your dreams. Leave the pen on the open, empty page. Your soul will love giving you something to write in the morning.

By paying attention to your dreams and learning to interpret their meaning, you can tap into a deep source of inner wisdom. Treat your dreams as a dialogue with your soul, and let them guide your path.

**You are never really alone.** Sometimes it is hard to connect with others and you feel separate and lonely. By paying attention to these signals and practicing mindfulness, you can strengthen your connection with your soul, spirit guides and passed loved ones and better understand the guidance being offered.

Even when someone passes and there feels a great distance between you, with you on Earth and your loved one in spirit, communication is possible. Loving one another and having a desire to connect increases the clarity. So saying, sadly nothing is guaranteed. You will most likely receive some messages but they may not always be from who you want to hear from. It took my late husband nine years to come and talk to me. I asked my guides why I was left alone for so long? The answer was that I was a very loyal wife. I was destined to marry again. The concern was that if my husband was in contact with me, I would not feel the desire to find another partner. I do agree that once contact was made, I did find a greater sense of peace. It had taken the painful feeling of loneliness to drive me back into the world. But the wonder of re-connecting was not just on my side. My husband was so excited he used to pop up at any possible opportunity. I was training to be a psychic medium. He used to regularly arrive in class to participate and became well known by my fellow students. He didn't just come and give me some messages but would arrive with loved ones associated with other students. When they struggled to communicate their messages, he would step in and give the message. It was like he was acting as a translator. The whole class used to laugh. We had great fun. I think the teacher was a little surprised.

When I speak to bereaved people, it never ceases to surprise me just how hard our passed loved-ones try to make contact with us. Craig Klugman PhD in his report of 2006 found that 62.6% of the participants in his study say they have been in contact with the dead. Most commonly, subjects reported Post Death Contacts that included dreams, sounds, feeling a presence, and having conversations.

## Tips for Recognising and Interpreting Signals

**Stay Open and Receptive**: Maintain an open mind and be receptive to subtle signals and signs.

**Meditate as often as you can**: Practice meditation to quiet your mind and enhance your intuitive abilities. In your meditation, try to sink deep within yourself. Usually, the deeper you go, the calmer you feel.

**Keep a Journal:** Record your experiences, dreams, and any signs you notice to help identify patterns and meanings. Sometimes a sign is not meaningful at the time but does become meaningful in the future.

I always date my journal entries so when I look back on them, it is easier to see if there are any patterns. In today's technological age, using MS Word or similar software it is possible to interrogate your journals using the word search functionality. I have looked for words like dad, family, dream, nature. This can sometimes reveal hidden insights. Such an example might be dad always visits when I have had a disagreement with my husband with advice on how I might have done things differently. In the future you might consult dad before the disagreement happens!

**Ask for Signs**: Actively ask your spirit guides for signs or guidance on specific issues. When you give them permission, it seems to make it easier for them to step forward and make contact.

**Trust Your Intuition**: Trust your inner feelings and insights when interpreting the signals you receive. Try using your intuition for small things first to help you to build trust in it. I often use my intuition to find lost items.

An example of where journalling helped my intuition was the knocking in our home in France. It is in a beautiful location and where I do most of my writing. We had hoped to take my lovely father-in-law to see it. Sadly, he passed before we got the opportunity to take him. When we moved in there was this persistent knocking in the attic over the sitting room. It is an old house and my partner thought perhaps the house was haunted. At the time I couldn't feel any presence so I put it down to the heat of the sun on the roof and walls. Sometime later when I was back in London, a psychic medium friend said she had a message for me. My father-in-law was trying to attract my attention in the French house. He wanted to say he had visited us there and loved the house. He could not get my partner and me to hear him so he had kept knocking in the hopes we would realise it was him. When I returned to France, I put my father-in-law's picture on the sideboard and told him we had received his message. We have never heard the knocking again.

I noted in my journal that I had not felt a presence. I wondered why I could not feel my father-in-law's presence when we heard the knocking. The response from my guide was that his message was focused on his son rather than me. Therefore, he radiated his energy towards my partner. It was why he noticed the knocking so much more than me. This message reassured me that my intuition was not playing tricks on me.

# 3

# Easy Steps to Connect with People in Spirit

**Here are three steps on how to proactively try to make contact with your spirit messengers.**

Before you try this, do ensure you have a quiet place to sit when you will not be interrupted. Close your eyes and try this;

1. **Reflect or meditate on the person** you wish to connect with taking some deep breaths to help you to relax. Remember your soul and guides are your friends and helpers. This connection is not a test but an exploration to be enjoyed. Regard it as like meeting an old friend after being apart for a while.
2. **Ask a simple question.** It is really important the question is

simple especially in the early days of making contact. The response may be as simple as feeling positive or negative about something, rather like a yes or a no. Over time you will develop the ability to receive and understand more detailed replies. Often this is with a sense of knowing.

3. **Wait for the response.** You may not receive all of your message at once. My students often get the headlines of their messages first and the detail arrives over the coming days. Surprisingly this often happens when they are doing something mundane like ironing or washing the car. Just remember your soul and guides are trying their hardest to reach you and will be creative on how they do it. All of this is made easier for both parties if you request contact.

Remember, in addition, it helps to do the following.

Be alert to receive the message in whatever way it chooses to arrive - the words of a song on the radio, a bill board, a knowing, a feeling..... all of the signs we discussed in the earlier chapter. Hearing words is the least common way of receiving a message. This often surprises people but sadly it's true.

*You will be amazed at the results.*

If you don't succeed the first time, try again another day. Don't try to filter whatever jumps into your head. Take it and write it down. It doesn't matter if it seems ridiculous or irrelevant. When you explore that fragment, you will receive more information. Filtering is the main cause for people saying they didn't get a reply

Whatever your situation is, and no matter how dire it may seem, remember – **you are never alone.**

## Tools you can use to assist with understanding your messages

Interpreting spirit messages can sometimes be challenging, as they often come in subtle, symbolic, or abstract forms. Fortunately, there are various tools and practices that can help you better understand and interpret the guidance you're receiving from your soul or spirit guides. Here's an overview of some of the most effective tools:

### Oracle Cards

Oracle cards are a popular and accessible tool for receiving and interpreting spirit messages.

- **How They Work**: Oracle cards are designed with images, symbols, and messages that can resonate with your intuition. When you draw a card, it often reflects the guidance or insight you need at that moment.
- **Using Oracle Cards**: To use oracle cards, set a clear intention or ask a specific question before shuffling the deck. Draw a card (or several) and reflect on the imagery and message. Pay attention to how the card's meaning aligns with your current thoughts, feelings, or situation. I found a three-card spread to be useful. The first card reflects looking backwards, the second where you are in your life when you drew the card, the third reflects potential futures.
- **Benefits**: Oracle cards offer a tangible way to connect with spirit messages and can provide clarity when you're uncertain about the meaning of a message.

There are many decks you can choose from. The ones I have

personally found useful are;

*The Spirit Messages: Daily guidance oracle deck by John Holland.* The reason I like this deck is that each card has a clear visual message and about six lines of narrative to go with it. I like the author's choice of blue butterflies on the back of the card. For me, the blue represents communication, and the butterfly is symbolic of transformation. It is a well-thought-through deck.

*The Soul's Journey: Lesson cards by James Van Praagh.* These cards have a mandala-style picture followed by a single-word headline, which may be sufficient for what you need to hear. The mandalas use sacred geometry and are similar to my soul maps. Your soul understands these pictures and the meanings of the shapes and colour used in them. If you need a little more information, please see the short message below. These cards I have found useful for guiding you on the headline of your message to set the context for the information you are seeing or feeling.

*Wisdom of Avalon: Oracle cards by Colette Baron-Reid.* These cards are full of symbology. The picture is bold and in the centre of the card, with a short headline and a few words below. If you find your spirit messengers like to work with symbols, a single card will give you much guidance. Draw a card, and allow your eyes to scan the card to see which elements of the picture jump out at you. Listen hard to your intuition to hear what message comes with this element of the card. Don't filter whatever comes into your mind. That is your message forming.

**Meditation**

Meditation is foundational for connecting with spiritual messages and understanding their meaning.

- **How It Works**: By quieting your mind and focusing inward, you create a receptive state where spirit messages can come through more clearly. During meditation, you might receive insights, images, or words that help decode the messages you've received.
- **Guided Meditation**: Using guided meditations specifically designed for spirit communication can also help you focus and tune in to the messages more effectively.
- **Benefits**: Meditation helps you connect with your intuition, providing a clearer channel for receiving and interpreting messages.

**Journalling**

Writing is a powerful tool for exploring and interpreting spiritual messages.

- **How It Works**: After receiving a message, spend time journaling about it. Write down the details of the message, how it made you feel, and any thoughts or insights that come up as you reflect on it. Journaling can help you make connections and uncover deeper meanings.
- **Automatic Writing**: This is a specific form of journaling where you allow yourself to write freely without conscious thought, letting your intuition or spirit guide provide the words. This can be an effective way to receive further guidance or clarity.
- **Benefits**: Journaling helps solidify your understanding and can reveal layers of meaning that might not be immediately apparent.

**Nature Walks**

Connecting with nature can help you interpret and understand spirit messages.

- **How It Works**: Spend time walking in nature with the intention of gaining clarity on a spirit message. As you walk, remain open to any signs, symbols, or intuitive thoughts that arise. The natural environment can often inspire or clarify spiritual insights.
- **Nature as a Mirror**: Nature has a way of reflecting back the messages we need to hear, whether through animals, weather patterns, or the serenity of the environment itself.
- **Benefits**: Nature walks help ground you and provide a peaceful setting for deeper reflection and connection with spirit messages.

In summary, understanding spirit messages is an intuitive and personal process, but with the help of tools like oracle cards, meditation, journaling and nature walks, you can gain greater clarity and confidence in interpreting the guidance you receive. These practices not only enhance your ability to connect with your spirit guides but also deepen your spiritual journey, helping you navigate life with more insight and assurance.

Lucid dreaming, especially when used with intentionality, is a powerful and advanced tool for understanding spirit messages and exploring your inner landscape. Incorporating lucid dreaming into your spiritual practice as a tool for understanding spirit messages is a powerful step. As you become more confident in your spiritual abilities, this advanced technique offers a deeper, more interactive way to explore and interpret the guidance you receive. While it requires dedication and practice, the insights gained from lucid dreaming can be transformative, providing clarity and understanding that goes beyond traditional methods of spiritual exploration.

## Healing resulting from the relationship you have with your spirit guides

Developing a relationship with your spirit guides can be profoundly healing on many levels—emotionally, mentally, and spiritually. Guides offer guidance, comfort, and wisdom that can lead to deep, transformative healing. Whether you are experiencing loneliness or seeking spiritual development, healing will assist your life's journey.

Here's how this relationship can bring about healing:

**Emotional Healing**

Spirit guides provide a constant source of unconditional love and support, which can be incredibly healing, especially during times of emotional distress. Knowing that you have a compassionate presence always available to you can alleviate feelings of loneliness, fear, and anxiety.

Spirit guides can gently help you to process and heal from past traumas. Continuing to carry these burdens alone can be very tough. Through their guidance, you may receive insights or find the strength to confront and release the emotional pain that has been holding you back.

Spirit guides often offer encouragement when you're facing challenges, reassuring you that you're on the right path. This emotional support can bolster your resilience and confidence, helping you to navigate life's difficulties with greater ease.

### Mental Healing

Spirit guides can help you gain clarity on situations that may be causing you mental stress or confusion. By offering a broader perspective; they can assist you in seeing things from a new angle, leading to a release of mental tension and overthinking.

Spirit guides can provide specific guidance on how to approach life's challenges, which can reduce anxiety and worry. When you trust in the wisdom of your spirit guides, you're more likely to feel mentally at peace, knowing you're being led in the right direction.

Spirit guides can also help you become aware of and transform negative thought patterns. By bringing these patterns to your attention, you can replace them with more positive and constructive ways of thinking.

### Physical Healing

While spirit guides do not replace medical advice, they can offer guidance that supports physical healing, such as encouraging you to adopt healthier habits, manage stress, or seek appropriate medical care. Their guidance often aligns with what is best for your body and overall well-being.

Spirit guides can also work with your energy body to support physical healing. For example, during meditation or energy healing sessions, you might feel their presence as they help to balance and restore your energy, which can have a positive impact on your physical health.

In summary, the relationship you have with your spirit guides can be a powerful source of healing, touching every aspect of your being. Whether you're seeking emotional comfort, mental clarity, spiritual growth, or even support for physical well-being, your spirit guides are there to offer guidance and healing tailored to your needs. This relationship not only helps you overcome challenges but also empowers you to live a life of greater peace, balance, and fulfilment.

## Build a stronger bridge with your soul and spirit guides

Creating a deeper and more consistent connection with your soul and spirit guides is a powerful way to enhance your spiritual journey. Building this bridge allows for clearer communication, more profound guidance, and a stronger sense of purpose and alignment in your life. Ideas for strengthening this connection include:

- **Cultivate Daily Spiritual Practices** such as meditation, prayer, journaling.
- **Develop Your Intuition** by learning to trust your inner voice and mindful observations of signs and synchronicities.
- **Create Sacred Space for Connection** – a corner of your home, an alter with meaningful objects such as a candle or crystals symbolising your spiritual connection. Regularly cleanse this space so it remains clean and positive to enhance your communication with your guides.
- **Ask for Guidance and Be Open to Receive.** Ask simple questions and be open to receiving a reply.
- **Consistency Is Key, and Trusting the Process.** Building a strong connection takes time and regular practice. Be patient with yourself and your spirit guides as you develop this relationship. Sometimes, the connection may feel strong, and at other times, it may feel distant. Trust that this is a normal part of the process and that the connection

is always there, even when it's not immediately apparent.

To summarise, building a stronger bridge with your soul and spirit guides is an ongoing journey that deepens with time, intention, and practice. By cultivating daily spiritual practices, developing your intuition, and creating sacred spaces, you open the channels for clearer communication and more profound guidance. This connection not only supports your spiritual growth but also helps you align more closely with your soul's purpose and navigate life with greater clarity and confidence.

# 4

# Meet Your Messenger

Your messenger will be either a passed loved one, your soul, one of your guides or perhaps an angel. The most likely angel being your Guardian Angel. Much as humans use faces to identify each other, each of your spirit messengers will have their own energetic feel. Many people find each messenger has their own way they like to make contact. In the beginning you will not know the difference between them. As long as they feel alright to you and you feel safe, you don't need to know which messenger it is. Over time you will start to discern between them. The most likely ones you will identify first will be passed loved ones. At an intuitive level you will already know how their energy feels from when they were with you on Earth. Usually, the next messenger you become familiar with is your main guide. They make the effort to spend time with you so they can almost become part of your everyday life.

From my earliest years I happily chatted to someone inside of me not knowing who they were. Knowing no difference, I assumed everybody else did too. Many children do the same until they are seven when the practice seems to fade. I was a sickly child and spent much of my time in bed. A simple cold would send me to bed for a week to wait for my immune system to kick in. Bored and a little lonely, I kept my practice of chatting to my internal friend going throughout my growing up and into my adult years.

My friend was always with me being my companion, nurturing and loving me. I knew I was never really alone. At a time of crisis, he directed me and at a time of upset he would comfort me. Why would I want to deny his existence as many parents encourage their children to do.

Connecting with a spirit messenger is often seen as a profound and transformative experience. However, your soul is an integral part of you and therefore with you when you are doing everyday things as well as when you are seeking to walk the spiritual path. Working as a team with your spirit messengers, there are inevitable upsets especially when you are struggling with doing something or you feel you have fallen short of what you wanted to achieve. My guides have always used humour wrapped in compassion to help us all get over these hurdles. In my experience my relationship with my guides is not pupil and school teacher but more like wisdom seeker and guide. My advice would be not to take yourself too seriously. Try to make the journey of your spiritual blossoming interesting, fun and rewarding. Accept that sometimes it feels like two steps forwards and one back. As you learn to communicate, there will be some misunderstandings on the messages you receive. This is one of the reasons why curiosity and a sense of humour are good companions on this journey.

In meeting and communicating with your spirit messenger, it is good to ground yourself, seek their help, and follow your intuition to guide you while maintaining a balanced perspective.

Let's look at approaches to aid your communications with your guides in a little more detail:

## Ground Yourself

Before attempting to connect with a spirit messenger, it's essential to ground yourself. Grounding helps you stay connected to the Earth and present in the moment. This ensures that your energy is stable and focused.

*Techniques for Grounding*: You can ground yourself through various methods such as deep breathing, meditation, visualising roots growing from your feet into the earth, or spending time in nature.

The purpose of grounding is to ensure that your energy remains balanced, making it easier to receive clear, authentic communication from your spirit messenger without interference from distractions or negative energies.

## Ask for Their Help

Once grounded, invite your spirit messenger to connect with you. This is done by setting a clear intention and asking for their guidance.

## Setting Intentions

Be specific about the kind of help or guidance you're seeking. You might ask for support in a particular area of your life or request general guidance for your spiritual journey.

## Openness and Trust

Approach this step with an open heart and trust that your spirit messenger will respond in a way that serves your highest good.

## Follow Your Heart

As you open yourself to communication, listen to your heart. Spirit messengers often communicate through subtle feelings, intuitions, or inner knowing.

*Heart-Centred Listening*: Pay attention to the feelings and insights that arise, especially those that resonate deeply with your core beliefs and values.

*Trusting Intuition*: Following your heart means trusting your intuition, even if the guidance you receive isn't immediately logical or conventional.

## Use Common Sense

While following your heart is important, it's equally crucial to use common sense. Spirit messages should resonate with practicality and align with ethical living. If it is not like this, it may be your ego interfering with the communication. If this happens, stop and try again another day.

## Practical Application

Consider how the guidance you receive can be applied in real-life situations. Does it make sense in the context of your life?

Not every message will be clear-cut or easy to interpret. This is not about blindly following what you perceive your guidance to be. Use your reasoning and judgment as well to discern the best course of action.

## Be Mindful of Your Ego

The ego can sometimes interfere with spiritual communication, leading to misinterpretations or a desire to control the outcome.

## Self-Reflection

Regularly check in with yourself to ensure that your ego isn't distorting the messages you receive. Are you hearing what you want to hear, or what you need to hear?

## Humility and Openness

Approach the experience with humility, recognizing that true guidance comes from a place beyond personal desires or fears.

In summary, meeting your spirit messenger involves a balance of spiritual openness and grounded practicality. By grounding yourself, asking for help, following your heart, using common sense, and being mindful of your ego, you create a pathway for clear and meaningful communication with your spirit messenger. This practice can lead to deeper spiritual insights, greater self-awareness, and more aligned decision-making in your life.

Greater insight into the relationship you have with your spirit messenger and the messages they give you often arrives over time. This was true for me. As an adult I explored my spiritual self and inner landscape, I came to believe my life companion was a spirit guide helping me to develop. It is only in my 60th decade that I realised my life companion, with whom I had shared all of my life's ups and downs, was my own soul. We had laughed together, cried together and worked together to overcome the life challenges we all get. I couldn't imagine life without him.

Increasingly people are asking me about their spiritual development and recognising their soul. I do it by just following my intuition. You don't have to make it difficult. Just do the 3 simple steps in the previous chapter – go inside by reflecting, simple question, wait for a response. Listen to your intuition, that feeling inside often around the heart. You can go a long way with your intuition.

# 5

# Your Messages Explained

Receiving spirit messages, whether through meditation, dreams, or intuitive insights, can be a profound experience. These messages often carry guidance, wisdom, or encouragement from your spirit guides or soul. To make the most of this communication, it's important to engage with the messages mindfully and intentionally. Here's how to approach and integrate your spirit messages:

## Write your messages down

When you receive a spirit message, whether it's a word, phrase, image, or feeling, it's crucial to write it down. It is very easy to forget the message. Also date when you first received it. Of course, the detail may expand or change over time.

**Documenting the Message**: Keep a dedicated journal or notebook where you record your spirit messages. Writing them down helps you capture the essence of the message while it's fresh in your mind and ensures you don't forget any details.

**Reflective Practice**: Writing also allows you to reflect on the message over time, noticing any recurring themes or patterns that may emerge.

I have experienced receiving the same message but years apart. However, the meaning I took from the message changed as my capabilities and awareness had grown. This is one of the reasons why I like to date and file my messages and review them periodically – often a New Year activity. In the review, I often have an 'Ah ha' moment understanding something which seems very obvious now but previously totally passed me bye.

## Your message may be revised in coming days

Spirit messages can be fluid and open to reinterpretation. As you live with the message, you might find that its meaning evolves or deepens.

**Ongoing Reflection:** Revisit your written messages in the days or weeks following their receipt. New insights or life experiences may shed additional light on the meaning of the message.

**Be Open to Change**: Understand that the interpretation of a spirit message isn't always immediate or final. Allow space for the message to grow and adapt to your unfolding journey.

## Laugh and relax

Engaging with spirit messages doesn't always have to be a serious or solemn experience. It's important to approach this practice with a sense of lightness and ease.

Laughing and relaxing can help you stay grounded and prevent overanalysing or stressing about the messages. Spiritual growth is as much about joy and ease as it is about insight.

Relaxing into the experience allows the messages to flow more freely, without the constraints of worry or overthinking.

I have come to love ironing our family laundry. It is a mundane and boring task but I have found I have some of my best conversations with my guide while I'm ironing. In a busy life it can be challenging to find quiet down time to meditate. In frustration, I feel my guides have taken to connecting while I'm ironing. It really isn't as silly as it sounds. My human brain is busy with the ironing and ensuring I don't get burnt in the process. Another part of me drifts off to have fun with my guides. The interaction can be about anything of theirs or my choosing or whatever happens to come up. There is no pre-defined agenda any more than there would be if you had a coffee and a chat with a friend. But if I am working on a project, such as this book, and I want their input, I have pen and paper with me to capture their ideas. If I don't make notes as it arrives, I find I lose the richness of the detail.

## Walk in nature on your messages

Nature provides a powerful backdrop for reflection and connection with your spirit messages.

Take your spirit messages with you on a walk in nature.

Walking in a natural setting can help you process and integrate the guidance you've received, grounding the spiritual into the physical world.

As you walk, you may find that the messages become clearer or that new insights emerge, inspired by the tranquility and wisdom of the natural environment.

Working in my garden in France or with my vegetable pots in London have been very productive for messages. There seems to be something very calming about having your hands in soil. As the calmness arrives so do my guides who love to drop in for a chat.

In summary, spirit messages are a valuable source of guidance and insight, offering a deeper connection to your spiritual path. By writing them down, remaining open to their evolving meanings, approaching them with humour and relaxation, and reflecting on them in nature, you can fully integrate these messages into your life. This practice not only deepens your spiritual awareness but also brings a sense of balance and harmony to your daily experiences.

# 6

# Setting Boundaries with Spirit Guides and Passed Loved Ones

Establishing clear boundaries in your spiritual practice is essential for maintaining a balanced and healthy relationship with spirit guides and passed loved ones. While these spiritual connections can provide guidance, comfort, and wisdom, it's important to ensure that these interactions happen on your terms and in a way that feels safe and manageable to you. Additionally, basic psychic protection is necessary to safeguard your energy from unwanted influences. Here's how you can set boundaries and protect yourself psychically.

## Setting Boundaries with Spirit Guides

Spirit guides are spiritual entities that offer guidance, protection, and insight. While they are typically benevolent, it's still important to set boundaries to ensure that your interactions remain positive and empowering. Ultimately this is your life and you are responsible for managing it. When you start to communicate or are in a key phase of development, I have seen spirit guides get overly excited. Receiving spirit messages at any time of the day or night is unacceptable. As a human you need sleep and down time to be healthy.

**Define the Terms of Communication**: Be clear about when and how you want your spirit guides to communicate with you. For example, you might set the intention that you only want to receive messages during meditation or specific times of the day.

**Limit the Frequency**: If you feel overwhelmed by constant communication, politely request that your spirit guides limit their interactions. For instance, you can ask them to step back if they are too present or to only communicate when you explicitly ask for their guidance.

**Respect Your Own Space**: Make it clear that your personal space, especially during times of rest or privacy, should be respected. You can set the intention that your spirit guides do not disturb you during sleep or personal moments.Connecting with passed loved ones can be comforting and healing, but it's important to set boundaries to prevent emotional overwhelm or unwanted intrusion.

## Setting boundaries with passed loved ones

Connecting with passed loved ones can be comforting and healing, but it's important to set boundaries to prevent emotional overwhelm or unwanted intrusion.

**Specify Times for Connection**: Like with spirit guides, determine specific times when you are open to connecting with passed loved ones. This could be during meditation, prayer, or a ritual designed for this purpose.

**Emotional Boundaries**: If you find that the presence of a passed loved one stirs up strong emotions, it's alright to ask them to step back until you're ready to engage. You might say, "I need some space right now, and I'll connect with you when I'm ready."

**Guided Interaction**: Use a trusted spiritual practitioner if you feel uneasy about direct communication. This can help maintain boundaries and ensure that the interaction is controlled and safe.

## The need for basic psychic protection

Psychic protection is crucial for maintaining your energetic integrity such as your thoughts and feelings, and protecting yourself from negative influences. Here are some of my favourites, but simple, means of protection.

**Visualise a Protective Barrier**: One common method of psychic protection is to visualize a protective shield around your body. The one I use with my students is to imagine a beautiful bubble of energy around you. You can choose the colour you would like such as iridescent pink, bright blue, verdant green or simply a wonderful white which contains all of the colours of the rainbow. You can be sure your soul is influencing the choice of colour. It will be just the right colour for where you are in your life at the time of choosing.

**Grounding Practices**: Regular grounding practices help anchor your energy to the Earth, making you less susceptible to spiritual or psychic interference. Grounding can be achieved through deep breathing, walking barefoot on the earth, or visualising roots extending from your feet into the ground.

**Set Clear Intentions**: State your intentions clearly that only positive, high-vibration energies are allowed in your space. You might say, "I welcome only positive energies and protect myself from any harm or negative influences."

**Use Protective Symbols**: Wearing or placing protective symbols around your home, such as the evil eye, pentagram, protective crystals can offer additional layers of protection.

When I have been working with a group, we always 'close down' at the end of the session. The session will have opened up our energies. So, when we have finished, we need to consciously close our energies down to protect them. You wouldn't dream of leaving home with your front door wide open for people to take what they want. It is much the same with your energy. As I am a belt and braces person, I ask everyone to ground themselves, close down their chakras and throw a ball of light around themselves that is a colour of their choice. Then I feel we are all safe to go about our business.

Setting boundaries with spirit guides and passed loved ones, as well as practicing basic psychic protection, are essential steps for maintaining your spiritual and emotional well-being. By defining clear terms of engagement, protecting your energy, and respecting your own limits, you create a safe and empowered space for spiritual connection. These practices ensure that your spiritual interactions are beneficial, supportive, and aligned with your highest good.

# 7

# Do I Truly Feel Supported by My Spirit Messengers?

Feeling supported by your spirit messengers, including your soul, spirit guides and passed loved ones, is a deeply personal and spiritual experience. It involves trust, self-awareness, and the ability to recognize and interpret the guidance and comfort they offer. The aim is to help you to achieve a balanced and happy life and alleviate any feelings of loneliness.

Let's explores how to discern the support you receive from the presence of passed loved ones, the wisdom within your soul, and the guidance provided by spirit guides.

## Presence of passed loved ones: Trust and familiarity

Passed loved ones often continue to offer support and love from the spiritual realm. It's important to remember that their essence remains the same, even though they are no longer in the physical world.

When I work as a psychic medium, I find grandparents play an important role in peoples' lives. They were guiding my sitters during their childhood and are much loved. A grandparent is often a confidant when life challenges can't so easily be shared with a parent. During a sitting, grandparents regularly arrive to give love and advice.

Just because your loved ones are now in the Afterlife, don't expect them to suddenly become different beings. The traits, personality, and love that defined them in life persist, making their presence familiar and comforting. You already know them, and this familiarity allows you to trust the guidance and comfort they provide.

A powerful example of this was with a student, Andrea, who felt a deep sense of support from her mother even after her passing. One day, while feeling particularly low on a train going to work, Andrea suddenly felt an overwhelming sensation of being hugged. It was as if her mother, who had always comforted her in life, was still there, wrapping her arms around her from the Afterlife. This experience reassured Andrea that her mother was still with her, offering love and support just as she had always done. Andrea had been feeling very lonely but was now so relieved she was not alone. She had to turn her head to the train window so no-one could see the tear that ran down her face. A few days later, Andrea was told by her guide how hard her Mum had worked to learn how to give the sensation of a physical hug. He was very proud of her.

## Discover your own wisdom held by your soul

While spirit messengers provide guidance, it's equally important to recognize the wisdom that already resides within you. Your soul holds deep knowledge and insight that can help you navigate life's challenges.

Sometimes, the support you seek from spirit messengers is already within you. By connecting with your soul through meditation, reflection, or journaling, you can access your own innate wisdom. This inner knowing can be a powerful guide in making decisions and finding peace in difficult situations.

Discovering and trusting your own wisdom empowers you to take control of your spiritual journey. While spirit messengers can guide you, the ultimate authority over your life's direction lies within you - you and your soul.

## Everyday Advice and Spiritual Development from Spirit Guides

Spirit guides are not just about spiritual growth. They are there to assist you in every part of your life, including practical everyday aspects of it. Spirit guides often provide subtle nudges or insights that can help with daily decisions, from navigating relationships to making career choices. This support can come in the form of intuitive feelings, synchronicity events, or inner voices that offer reassurance or warning.

I feel it is when you let your soul and guide into your everyday life, that you cease to feel so alone. There is someone to consult whenever you need them. One of my colleagues really does this.

One evening after a presentation at a conference, I met him at the exit as everyone was filing out. He had paused at the doorway and I asked him if he was alright. To my surprise he said he was just asking his guide where his friend was as they wanted to meet up to go for a drink. He had obviously received his instructions as a second later he was walking purposely off.

Beyond everyday advice, spirit guides are also there to help you evolve spiritually. They might guide you toward experiences or knowledge that will expand your consciousness, deepen your understanding of the universe, and foster your spiritual growth.

Feeling supported by your spirit messengers is about recognising the various ways in which they offer guidance and comfort. Whether it's the familiar presence of passed loved ones, the deep wisdom held by your soul, or the practical and spiritual guidance from spirit guides, these connections can provide a profound sense of support and direction. By trusting in these spiritual relationships and the wisdom within, you can navigate life's challenges with greater confidence and peace.

# 8

# Break Through Barriers Holding You Back in Life

Even with spirit messages providing comfort and guidance, there are several barriers that can challenge your ability to move your life forward. Just knowing about them can help you to acknowledge if you are experiencing it and to find strategies for overcoming it. Below, we'll explore these barriers through various lenses, including real-life stories, emotions, and principles.

## Fear and Forgiveness

Fear is a powerful emotion that can paralyse a person, preventing them from making necessary changes or moving forward.

This fear is often tied to past traumas or unresolved issues, such as a painful divorce.

Consider a friend who went through a divorce after discovering her partner's infidelity. The initial fear of being alone, the uncertainty about the future, and the anger towards her partner kept her stuck. She struggled to forgive him, not realising that forgiveness was less about absolving him of guilt and more about freeing herself from the chains of resentment.

Once she embraced forgiveness, her life began to move forward. She was able to release the fear that was holding her back, and she started to rebuild her life, opening herself up to new possibilities. The guidance from her spirit messengers, who offered support and reassurance, helped her understand that holding onto anger only hurt herself and that forgiveness was a key to her healing.

## Judgment Versus Truth

Judgment is another barrier that can distort one's perception of reality. When you judge yourself or others harshly, you may fail to see the truth of a situation. Judgment is often based on fear, insecurity, or societal conditioning, and it can lead to feelings of unworthiness or superiority.

For example, you might judge someone else's life choices without knowing their full story, or you might judge yourself harshly for past mistakes. Spirit messengers often encourage us to look beyond judgment and seek the truth. The truth is liberating, as it allows you to see situations and people (including yourself) more clearly, without the cloud of preconceived notions.

Letting go of judgment requires honesty, self-reflection, and the willingness to see things as they truly are. It allows you to align more closely with your true self and make decisions that are in your best interest.

## Anxiety and Anger About Death

Death is a natural part of life, but it can evoke intense emotions like anxiety and anger. These emotions often stem from fear of the unknown, unresolved grief, or the feeling that life is unfair.

The guidance from spirit messengers can help ease these feelings by reminding us that death is not an end but a transition. Passed loved ones may communicate messages of peace, love, and reassurance, helping to soothe the anxiety and anger surrounding death.

For instance, someone who lost a close family member might struggle with the unfairness of the loss. They may feel anger towards life or even towards the deceased for leaving them behind. However, through spiritual guidance, they can come to understand that their loved one is still with them in spirit, offering support and love from beyond. This understanding can help them find peace and acceptance, allowing them to move forward with their life.

## Critical Inner Voice

Compassion and self-love are essential for personal growth and healing. However, they are often overlooked or undervalued. Many people struggle with self-compassion, instead being their harshest critics. Your ego can be a strong inner critical voice trying to wrestle back control of your life by interfering with your communications with your soul and spirit guides. If this happens stop, ask the critical voice to be quiet and try connecting again on another day.

It is important to treat yourself with the same kindness and understanding that you would offer to a friend. This includes recognizing your own worth, forgiving yourself for past mistakes, and allowing yourself to feel and heal.

When you cultivate self-compassion, you create a space for healing and growth. Spirit messengers often encourage this practice, reminding us that we are deserving of love and kindness, both from ourselves and from others. As you learn to love yourself, you open the door to greater spiritual connection and guidance.

## Inability to Remain in the Here and Now

Living in the present moment is crucial for spiritual growth and personal fulfilment. However, many people get caught up in regrets about the past or anxieties about the future, which prevents them from fully experiencing the present.

Spirit messengers often emphasis the importance of staying grounded in the "here and now." The present moment is where life unfolds, and it is where you have the power to make changes and create your future. By focusing on the present, you can let go of past regrets and future worries, allowing yourself to fully engage with life as it is.

Practices like mindfulness and meditation can help you stay present and connected to your spiritual guidance. When you remain in the here and now, you are more open to receiving messages and insights from your spirit guides, which can help you navigate life's challenges with greater clarity and peace.

## It's a Relationship and Grows with Attention

Your connection with spirit messengers is like any other relationship—it requires time, attention, and nurturing. If you neglect this connection, it may weaken or fade over time. However, if you actively cultivate it, the relationship will grow stronger, offering more guidance and support.

This relationship can be nurtured through practices like meditation, prayer, or simply talking to your spirit guides as you would a trusted friend. The more you engage with them, the more attuned you become to their messages and guidance.

Remember, spirit messengers are always there to help, but the relationship is a two-way street. As you invest time and energy into this connection, you will find that it becomes a valuable source of support, wisdom, and love in your life.

In summary, moving your life forward often requires addressing various barriers, such as fear, judgment, anxiety, and a lack of self-compassion. By working through these challenges and maintaining a strong connection with your spirit messengers, you can overcome obstacles, find peace, and live a more fulfiling life.

# 9

# Transform Solitude into Personal and Spiritual Growth

Turning solitude into personal and spiritual growth can be a profound journey, leading to a fulfiling and purposeful life. It involves deep self-discovery, cultivating your gifts, reconnecting with joy, forming authentic relationships, and maintaining curiosity about your life. Doing all of these things will leave no space for feelings of loneliness. You will have built a strong foundation to your life from which you can led a happy and fulfiled life. When I was widowed, I thought I had a strong foundation but it turned out not to be strong enough to weather widowhood. I had to do some work to get to the life I desired.

Let's explore these life foundation building activities in more detail, incorporating real-life stories to illustrate the transformative power of solitude and spiritual guidance.

## Discover You & Be Your Authentic Self

Alexia's journey toward authenticity was shaped by two very different marriages. Her first husband was supportive and encouraged her to explore her spiritual side. It was during this marriage that Andrea began to open up to the idea of spirit guides and messengers. She started meditating, journaling, and listening to her intuition. These practices helped her uncover her true self—her passions, desires, and spiritual gifts. However, while her husband supported her spiritual exploration, the relationship lacked the depth she craved, and she felt something was missing.

After their amicable divorce, Alexia met her second husband, who was quite different. He was intellectually rigorous, often challenging her thoughts and views. This was initially frustrating for Alexia, as it seemed to disrupt the spiritual harmony she had cultivated. However, over time, she realized that his challenges were a catalyst for her growth. He pushed her to question not only her spiritual beliefs but also the authenticity of her identity. This relationship forced her to confront her fears, insecurities, and the parts of herself that she had been avoiding.

Through this process Alexia discovered that being her authentic self, meant she had to embrace both her spiritual side and her intellectual curiosity. She learned to balance these aspects, becoming a more integrated and whole person. By facing the challenges in her relationship head-on, she was able to grow in ways she hadn't anticipated, ultimately finding a deeper sense of purpose and fulfilment.

## Cultivate Your Gifts—Both Practical and Spiritual

Cultivating your gifts involves recognising and nurturing both your everyday talents and your spiritual abilities. Practical gifts could include skills like writing, cooking, or problem-solving, while spiritual gifts might involve intuition, empathy, or healing.

For instance, Alexia had always been a skilled communicator, but she had never considered this a gift until she began working on her spiritual development. Through meditation and connecting with her spirit guides, she realised that her ability to communicate was not just a practical skill but also a spiritual gift. She started using her communication skills to help others, offering guidance and support to friends and strangers alike.

By cultivating both her practical and spiritual gifts, Alexia was able to live a more integrated and fulfiling life. She found that her gifts complemented each other, creating a harmonious balance that allowed her to serve others while also enriching her own life.

## Finding Your Way Back to Joy in the Moment

Finding joy in the moment often begins with self-awareness and self-compassion. For Alexia, after the challenges of her second marriage, she went through a period of deep introspection. She spent time alone, reconnecting with the things that brought her joy—reading, painting, and spending time in nature. She learned to appreciate the small moments of happiness that came from being fully present in her life.

As Alexia healed and grew more comfortable with herself, she began to share her joy with others. She found that when she was genuinely happy and present, she naturally attracted others who were also seeking joy and connection. This led to the formation of new friendships and deepened her existing relationships.

By finding joy within herself first, Alexia was able to bring that joy into her interactions with others, creating a positive feedback loop that enriched her life and the lives of those around her.

## Meet People Who Like the Authentic You

When you embrace your authentic self, you naturally attract people who resonate with the real you. These are individuals who share similar interests, values, or life experiences, and who appreciate you for who you truly are.

After her spiritual and personal growth journey, Alexia found that the people she attracted into her life were different from those she had previously known. These new friends were more aligned with her true self—they shared her interests in spirituality, personal growth, and authentic living. They were not just friends; they were kindred spirits who supported her on her journey and helped her continue to grow.

These authentic relationships brought Alexia a sense of belonging and connection that she had never experienced before. She realised that when you are true to yourself, you create space for others who are also on a similar path to enter your life.

## Continue to Be Curious About Yourself and Your Life

Curiosity is a powerful tool for personal and spiritual growth. It keeps you open to new experiences, ideas, and opportunities for learning. Alexia's journey didn't stop after she found her authentic self; she continued to explore new interests and passions, which in turn brought new spirit guides into her life.

Alexia's experience was that as her interests grew, her main guide introduced her to new guides. This way of working with spirit seems to resonate with many spiritual traditions and beliefs. Spirit guides can enter our lives to assist us with specific tasks, challenges, or phases of growth is deeply rooted in various spiritual practices across cultures. Let's delve into some key perspectives on this phenomenon.

**Spirit Guides as Specialists**

In many spiritual traditions, spirit guides are seen as specialised beings who possess unique wisdom, skills, or knowledge in certain areas. As individuals embark on new endeavours or seek to deepen their understanding of particular subjects, it is believed that guides with expertise in those areas may step forward to offer their assistance.

For example, when Alexia began writing about spiritual topics, her primary guide introduced her to an ancient Chinese author. This suggests that this spirit guide had specific expertise in the art of writing and could assist you in expressing complex spiritual ideas through the written word.

Similarly, a guide connected with the time of Pharaoh Akhenaten came forward as you explored themes of life purpose, and healing—areas where this guide's experience and knowledge could be particularly beneficial.

**Evolution of the Soul's Journey**

As you progress on your spiritual journey, your needs and challenges evolve, and so do the types of guidance you require. The arrival of new guides can be seen as a reflection of your soul's growth and the new chapters in your spiritual path. Each new guide brings different energies, teachings, and perspectives that are necessary for the next stage of your journey.

Alexia's experience suggests a dynamic relationship with the spiritual realm, where your guides are not static but rather fluid, responding to your evolving needs. This also implies that you have an active role in attracting and working with these guides, as your intentions, interests, and focus shift over time.

In summary, turning solitude into personal and spiritual growth is a journey of self-discovery, authenticity, and continuous learning. By embracing solitude, you create space for deep reflection, allowing you to discover your true self and cultivate your unique gifts. This journey involves reconnecting with joy, forming authentic relationships, and maintaining an open and curious mind.

# 10

# Resources

Cheat Sheet for connecting and conversing with your spirit messengers

| Action | Action Title | Summary Guidance |
|---|---|---|
| | | |
| **Phase 1: Pre- request for connection with your spirit messengers** | | |
| 1 | **Reflect on your question** | This could be something like – what feels good for me? Or simply, can you hear me? |
| 2 | **Be alert to simple signals in your everyday life.** | This could be the starting point of your connection and help you to frame your question. |
| 3 | **Find a quiet space and time to talk to your spirit messengers.** | |
| 4 | **Ground yourself** | The easiest way to do this is to visualise roots coming out of the souls of your feet. |
| | | |
| **Phase 2: Session to connect with your spirit messengers** | | |
| 1 | **Reflect or meditate on the person you wish to connect with.** | Taking some deep breaths can help you to relax. |
| 2 | **Ask a simple question** | At the beginning try to ask yes/no questions and sense if the response is positive or negative. When you have practised this, move on to asking a bigger question but not too big. |
| 3 | **Wait for the response** | You may get only headlines initially. More detail can arrive in the coming days. |
| | | |
| **Phase 3: Post conversation with your spirit messengers** | | |
| 1 | **Keep a journal** | This can capture signals, messages from sessions, dreams etc |
| 2 | **Be open to receiving more information** | Request that it is for the highest good of all. |
| 3 | **Follow your heart** | Pay attention to feelings and insights that rise from your heart |
| | | |

# 11

# Keeping the Game Alive

Now you have everything you need to connect with your passed loved ones, soul, and spirit guide, it's time to pass on your new found knowledge and show other readers where they can find the same help.

Simply by leaving your honest opinion of this book on Amazon, you'll show other people experiencing loneliness where they can find the information they're looking for, and how they might move their life forward.

Thank you for being so helpful. The ability to *Never Feel Alone* is kept alive when we pass on our knowledge – and you're helping us to do just that.

You can leave a review of *Never Feel Alone* on Amazon here or scan

Or, if you prefer, send me an email with your honest feedback to alison.wem@yoursoulfamily.com .

Thank you so much for your help.

Love and Light,
Alison

YOUR SOUL FAMILY

Read Alison's blog here
Sign up for Alison's newsletter here

**As a thank you for being among the first to read Never Feel Alone – please get your FREE copy of my earlier book**
***Creating Your Soul Map.*** **Try introducing yourself to your soul.**
**Creating Your Soul Map – FREE bonus**

www.yoursoulfamily.com

# 12

# Conclusion

***Never Feel Alone*** is a comprehensive guide aimed at helping individuals cultivate a deeper connection with their soul and spirit guides. It provides practical advice and spiritual insights to overcome feelings of loneliness and isolation by fostering a relationship with the spiritual realm.

Getting to know your authentic self assists you in attracting people into your life who relate to the real you. In so doing, you work yourself out of loneliness into a life full of purpose and the people who truly relate to you.

The book emphasizes that every person has the innate ability to connect with both earthly and spiritual beings, which can bring profound support, companionship, and guidance.

## Key Topics and Conclusions

**Life's Challenges and Loneliness**

The book acknowledges that challenges, including loneliness, are a natural part of life. However, it stresses that how you respond to loneliness defines who you are now or who you choose to become. You have the power to change your experience of loneliness by shifting your perspective and actions.

**Empowerment to Change**

If you find yourself unhappy with being alone, the book encourages you to recognise that the ability to change your situation lies within you. The journey towards overcoming loneliness begins with the decision to embrace change and seek connection, whether with yourself, others, or the spiritual realm.

You might think these things are easier said than done. As a widow I had no adult social life which was driving my sense of loneliness. I felt unable to go out socially or give a dinner party on my own.

In pure frustration, I decided to give a dinner party for widows and widowers. It felt like safe ground as they would appreciate my fears and challenges of being both the hostess and the cook without my husband by my side. To help alleviate my overwhelm, I picked a good-natured widower and asked him to host giving out drinks as people arrived. This gave me the time to deal with the finishing touches for dinner. As the corks popped everyone relaxed and started to chat and laugh. Dinner for eight is no mean feat to achieve on your own. At last adult laughter had returned to my home. It was a pivotal moment in my recovery from widowhood. From that dinner I received social invites out. It was from those invites I met my current partner. As the saying goes, the rest is history.

Taking yourself on this journey could feel easier said than done but it is doable. As a widow I had no adult social life which was driving my sense of loneliness. I felt unable to go our socially or to give a dinner party on my own. In pure frustration, I decided to give a dinner part for widows and widowers. It felt like safe ground as they would appreciate my fears and challenges of being both the hostess and the cook. To help alleviate my overwhelm, I picked a good-natured widower and asked him to host giving our drinks as people arrived. This gave me the time to deal with the finishing touches for dinner. As the corks popped everyone relaxed and started to chat and laugh. Dinner for eight is no mean feat to achieve on your own. At last adult laughter had returned to my home. It was a pivotal moment in my recovery from widowhood. From that dinner I received social invites out. It was from those invites I met my current partner. As the saying goes, the rest is history.

**Support from the Universe**

The universe is portrayed as a supportive force, offering various means to help you transform your circumstances. Whether through synchronicity, signs, or the presence of spirit guides, there is always spiritual assistance available to those who seek it.

**The Human Body as a Communication Technology**

One of the central ideas is that the human body itself is a powerful tool for communication. Intuition is likened to a radio receiver and sender, enabling you to send and receive messages not just with people on earth, but also with those in the

Afterlife. The book shares real-life stories, such as one involving a connection with a deceased mother, to illustrate how these communications can be both meaningful and transformative.

**Connection is Your Birthright**

The guide emphasizes that isolation and loneliness are not your natural state. You were born with the capacity to connect deeply with others, both in this world and beyond. This connection is a fundamental part of your being, designed to help you navigate life's challenges with the support of others and the spiritual realm.

Ultimately, the book's core message is that you are never truly alone. By cultivating a relationship with your soul, spirit guides and passed loved ones you can access a source of constant companionship, advice, and encouragement. This connection can provide solace in times of loneliness and empower you to live a life filled with purpose and connection.

"Never Feel Alone" serves as both a spiritual guide and a practical handbook, offering readers the tools and insights needed to develop a strong connection with the spiritual world, thereby overcoming feelings of loneliness and finding comfort in the support of the universe and beyond.

# Epilogue

For such a simple act which you were born to be able to do, connecting with your spirit guides and passed loved ones, there seems quite a lot of things to think about. But much like riding a bicycle; the first time can be hard but once you have started forward on the bicycle and stayed upright, you are off and going. There is no looking back.

Give it a go and see what happens....

If you have any questions or struggle to hear a reply from your spirit messengers, send me an email alison.wem@yoursoulfamily.com I will try to help you.

# About the Author

After a successful corporate career balanced with raising a family, Alison Wem left her job to pursue her true dream of helping people lead happier, healthier and more prosperous lives.

Alison is a spiritual teacher and offers creative workshops, classes and consultations in spiritual development, dreams, healing and psychic mediumship. Alison is renowned for helping people to get know their soul family and to experience connecting with their soul, spirit guides and passed loved ones. She is an author of a number of books on the topic.

Alison moved forward from widowhood to find an inner strength and wisdom she did not know she possessed. She did this through going within, the subject of her book series *Your Soul Family.*

Alison is married with five grownup children who have all flown the nest

**You can connect with me on:**

https://www.yoursoulfamily.com

https://www.facebook.com/AlisonWem

**Subscribe to my newsletter:**

http://eepurl.com/duDSXT

# Also by Alison Wem

**Creating Your Soul Map: Move beyond a challenge - connect with your soul for calmness, harmony, wisdom to find strength, love and guidance.**

A Soul Map is a picture of you and your life showing the important people in your life and your relationships with them.

As the name implies, it is also a route back to your soul where you will find love and guidance.

A short easy to read book with 7 simple steps to create your Soul Map. It's a good book if you are just setting out on your spiritual journey or feeling stressed with 21st century life.

**Secrets of Your Soul: A Story of Past Lives Unveils Personal Wisdom Beyond Your Wildest Dreams**

A story of past lives shows the everyday path to enlightenment all of us are walking whether we know it or not.

A gentle read which explores the wider reality of life beyond the life you are living today.

It helps you to realise there is purpose to your life and to assist in recognising your own wisdom.

**Finding Your Soul Family: A Guide to connecting with your soul to better understand your spiritual path**

Looks in more depth at your Soul Map to reveal the challenges in your life and to help you overcome them.

Become the observer of your life rather than the victim to learn your life lessons more easily and move your life forwards.

There is a discussion which explores if you are an eternal being living a life in a physical body.

Printed in Great Britain
by Amazon

51982993R00050